PRAISE FOR LETTERS TO THE FIRST LADY

This is an excellent read for not only first ladies, but all women. You will get a glimpse of the life and the sacrifice of a woman given the title "First". Women who have been given responsibility with no manual or instructions, and at the same time be willing to sacrifice their lives.

Letters to the First Lady will refresh, revive, recharge, and refocus your outlook on womanhood. There is a blessing in store for the world when women are given a platform to be heard and understood. For many who face challenges that are common among women in leadership, expect to be edified as you are instructed by others who have encountered major challenges.

— TAMMI WILLOUGHBY

&

Tammi Willoughby is the First Lady of More Life Worship Center in Sacramento, California. She is also the Principal and Administrator of More Life Christian Academy.

LETTERS TO THE FIRST LADY

DEVOTIONAL FOR PASTORS' WIVES AND WOMEN
MARRIED TO MINISTRY LEADERS

TÁMU BLUE MILLER

Lady Ashan Alamin,
Thank you for your support.
God bless you.
Keep Shining!

Támu Blue M

Editing by EBM Professional Services
Artwork by LaShonda Willis-Wells
Cover image by BluPrint Private Brand Consulting
Book design by Rooted in Writing

First Printing, 2020

ISBN print: 978-1-7348022-0-7

To contact the author about this book, email her at shinediamondllc@outlook.com.

To my Mema, the late Dr. Patricia Joseph. I miss you so much, Momma. I will carry on your legacy through education, ministry, and writing. I hope I continue to make you proud.

I've been inspired by many first ladies, but will only name a few. Thank you to Lady Alice Williams, Lady Ethel Foster, Lady Tammi Willoughby, Lady Serita Jakes, and the late Lady Dr. Lois Evans. You have shown what grace under fire looks like. You will and have come forth as pure gold.

ACKNOWLEDGMENTS

Lord, I couldn't have done this without You. Thank You for entrusting me with this endeavor. I am honored that You would use me. All glory and honor belongs to You.

To my husband and best friend, Neal Jr. Thank you for believing in me, pushing me, loving me, and covering me in prayer. You are the best. I love you!

To my son, Neal III and my daughter, Nyla. You inspire me to be better. I am extremely proud to be your mother. I love you both very much!

To the contributors:

Ladies, thank you for trusting me enough to share your stories. I admire each and every one of you. Praying God's best over you and your future accomplishments.

CONTENTS

INTRODUCTION

There is a great anointing on your husband's life. His calendar may be filled with invitations to minister around the world, yet some may start to become interested in his personal life. Many may say, "Whoever is married to this man is blessed." A search begins to see who the first lady is in his life, as his followers inquire more about the woman he has chosen. "How does she look? Do they make a good match?"

Unfortunately, some are not curious in truly getting to know the first lady. These troublemakers are only concerned with her appearance and setting unrealistic demands on her. Some may even diminish this office to just a title and nothing more.

Oh, but Dear First Lady, you are so important. Even though the leader in your life is constantly in the spotlight, receiving tremendous accolades and compliments, your private prayers, support, shoulder to cry on, and listening ear is what helps make your leader become the best that he can be. Some may not see your value, but trust that God and your leader does.

You are the first lady in his life. You are the first to see the core of your husband. You are the woman that prays and builds him up through disappointments, frustration, and challenges. You are also his safe place where he feels comfortable. He feels at home whenever you are with him. Others may only celebrate the gift placed in him, but his first lady honors the man, husband, father, son, and brother that God created him to be.

I heard a story about how a pastor and his wife were out running errands. They went to a store where they saw an old boyfriend of the pastor's wife. The pastor said to his wife, "Look at how he turned out. Aren't you glad you married me instead of him?"

Her response was, "If I would have married him, he would be a pastor." In other words, the pastor had to recognize that he wouldn't be who he is without his first lady.

I have a heart for pastors' wives and women married to ministry leaders.

Your husband was called.

You have been called as well.

My prayer is to continue seeing you appreciated, loved, adored, rested, anointed, and living out your purpose.

I believe a great sacrifice comes along with being a first lady, and God has equipped you with all that is required to walk in this office. Yet there are instances when a personal time of respite is crucial—to reset naturally and physically in order to continue being effective.

The purpose of this book is for you to be encouraged and strengthened by stories of women who share the same experiences as you. You will be surprised by how much you have in common. Most of these beautiful, strong, and brave women are currently married or have been married to a pastor or ministry leader. My prayer is that this book will be an outlet for you to see that you are not alone.

Dear First Lady, be refreshed.

WOMAN TO WOMAN

*D*ear First Lady,
   I noticed how the lady in the tight, bright red dress came up to the altar so that Bishop could lay hands. Girl, I wanted to tell her, "Go sit down somewhere. I see you, and your intentions are suspicious." But nevertheless, like a queen, you graciously stood in your place. Knowing this wasn't the first time this has happened, I whispered this prayer with you in mind, "Lord, cover and strengthen her husband as you deliver the soul of this woman."

Your husband is constantly in the spotlight. Because your husband is in the spotlight, some women will see and identify him as a symbol of power. Without good prudence and dignity, these women shamelessly hunger for it. All they see is your husband, and without regard for your family, these women will stop at nothing to get close to him.

When this happens, resist the temptation of comparing yourself to other women. Yes, there are other attractive women around him. There is always going to be someone who looks better than you, has more degrees than you, makes more money than you. But do you know who they are not? They are not YOU. No one can do the things you do and the special way you do them. Your husband loves you. Every part of you.

If your self-esteem is not where it should be, work on it. Speak the Word over yourself. Speak it until you believe it. Speak it until you walk in it. Life and death are in the power of the tongue. Build up your confidence. You have to do the work. If you're not happy with your appearance, do something about it. Do you need to change up your wardrobe? Do you need to add exercise to your daily routine? Do whatever is necessary for you to learn how to love yourself inside and out.

Do not rely on your husband or anyone else to build you up. A person can tell you how beautiful you are all day, but if you don't believe it for yourself, every affirmation given to you will be null and void.

Therefore, do not place that responsibility on those around you. No one should be filling your cup so that you feel good about yourself. To place this kind of task on man is unfair because they were never created to carry this kind of load. Man will fail you every time because of human limitation. God is the only one who can fill your cup as you read and meditate on the Word and His promises.

One of the many negative side-effects of insecurity is falsely accusing your husband of things that have not taken place or accusing him of behaviors that may have never crossed his mind. Be aware of where those accusations are coming from. Do not let the enemy plant seeds of discord in your mind to destroy your marriage. Do a self-check, pray, and even have a heart-to-heart discussion about your thoughts and feelings with your husband. Find the root of the problem and deal with it.

Be sure to make your presence known. If possible, show up at different speaking engagements. My husband would tell me how women sometimes complimented him on an item he was wearing and his response was, "Thank you. My wife bought it for me." It may be that your husband is oblivious to the advances of other women. Husbands are so busy ministering, smiling, and shaking hands, they don't see the signs. That is why it is very important that you cover your husband in prayer and connect with him intimately.

"What therefore God hath joined together, let not man put asunder."

— MARK 10:9 KJV

"Casting all your care upon him; for he careth for you."

— I PETER 5:7 KJV

"The LORD will perfect that which concerneth me: thy mercy, O LORD, endureth for ever: forsake not the works of thine own hands."

— PSALM 138:8 KJV

Lord, thank You for Your love and for keeping every promise. Thank You for tending to our cares and concerns. Thank You for reminding us through Your Word that we are fearfully and wonderfully made, we are the head and not the tail, we are a holy nation, we are more than conquerors, and that greater is in us because we have You. We cast down anything that exalts itself against the knowledge of God. We are special because we have been made in Your image and likeness. Thank You for loving us and teaching us to love ourselves and others. We love You, Lord. In Jesus' name. Amen.

TÁMU MILLER

LOVE

*D*ear Lady in Christ,

Are people constantly bringing things to your attention? "Did you hear about Brother So and So?" "I can't believe she wore *that* to church." "Where are your kids?" Do people ask your husband, "Where's your wife?" How do you respond? Sometimes I wonder why they are bothering me with that in the first place.

I was taught that God holds me accountable for my response towards others in spite of how I am treated. It really is all about love, my sister. The Bible tells us to love God and to love one another. It seems so simple and straightforward. But then reality hits—personalities, social media, daily schedules, work, stress, family, and, of course, church. Sometimes we get off track, but the scripture reminds us that,

> *"Charity suffereth long, and is kind . . . Beareth all things, believeth all things, hopeth all things, endureth all thing . . . Charity never faileth . . ."*
>
> — I CORINTHIANS 13:4, 7, 8 KJV

Love is the underlying current in all that we do in church, out of church, at home, at school, and at work.

As I pray, I ask the Lord to give me the words to say to His people. I ask Him to help me to season my words, and to help me as I go before the people. I know that if it were up to my flesh and not the Holy Spirit, I would lose my temper and say the wrong thing. Prayer really works. Oftentimes, the Lord tells me to hold my peace. I believe that He will fight our battles. By just waiting a moment, or an hour, or even a day, allows time for God to work. When people bring things to us, they generally have had ample time to think, but they still require an immediate response from us. Don't get caught up in the moment. Everything will work out. Wait on the Lord for what to do. He will work it out.

Finally, my sister, have a loving heart. Whenever people ask silly questions or they are always worrying about what someone else is doing or wearing, remember, love is kind. It hopes for the best and never fails. Consider human frailty and be thankful for the grace and strength that God gives us to overlook the things that can distract us from our purpose. This is how you love God and His people.

Love,

SIS. CARLA HAMILTON

FAMILY: YOUR FIRST MINISTRY

*H*ello First Lady,

I saw how upset you were last week when your family's plans were once again turned upside down. I know the family is well taken care of even though you have to take a back seat to your husband's calling and his job. I am sure this is especially hard since you don't make family plans often.

When you do make plans, your husband already has something on the calendar that you didn't know about or expect. As a result, it makes you angry because his plans never really include you or the children. Nevertheless, you don't want to be angry and start a fight that will provoke you to say something you'll regret. Words can't be taken back. Once they are out, they're out.

Oftentimes it feels like he doesn't care about what you want. It's like it's his way or the highway. You still need to respectfully make your feelings known and remind him of what you expect in a manner that he understands. God ordained marriage, and He wants His children to be happy. When neither of you are willing to change your plans, be prayerful because God is not the author of confusion. You want to make time for all the milestones in your lives that should be enjoyed by the family.

Though you feel all alone, remember that deep down inside he's trying to figure out a way for things to flow smoothly. To be honest, sometimes he is not going to try to fix it, because he's doing what he wants to do. He really does hate to see you upset though. Most of the time you are the one changing and rearranging your schedule because you don't want to be disobedient to God. God gave you good organizational skills. Remember when you are working in your gift, you will always be in His will. Keep praying. It will be fine.

Always keep that open line of communication between you and your spouse. Don't allow your frustrations to pile up and then speak out of anger. Take a breath. Pray and then talk in a calm and respectful manner. Your husband loves you and values your input. Even though the final decision will be his.

I remember my husband and I had a disagreement. He felt strongly about his opinion as did I. Instead of fussing about the situation, I prayed and laid it all out before the Lord. Before I knew it, my husband had changed his mind and agreed to go with my suggestion. I was thankful not only because we made the best choice for our family, but that I had a partner in life that had a heart sensitive to God's nudging. There will still be times when your husband will make a decision you're not fond of. Just know that ultimately, God's plan will succeed and there will always be a lesson to be learned.

"Many are the plans in a person's heart, but it is the Lord's purpose that prevails."

— PROVERBS 19:21 NIV

Father, in the name of Jesus, I ask You to cover these ladies and equip them with Your power to accomplish the job You have assigned them. Lord, give them discernment to know what to do when it needs to be done. Lord, thank You again. In Jesus' name. Amen.

APRIL COLEMAN

AS YOUR DAY

*D*ear Musician's Wife,

We march to the beat of a different drum. Our spouses are the musicians, but we are the conductors. Let me know if this "sheet music" sounds remotely familiar. Friday is finally here. You rush home to pick up the kids, make dinner, change clothes, and rush back out the house to church.

On the way there, while the kids are snacking, in bumper-to-bumper traffic, your cell phone rings. Your husband, who is also on his way to church, left his wallet at home and wants you to go back and get it. You think to yourself, *Oh no. If I go back, that's it! I'm not coming back out.*

But the Holy Ghost reminds you,

"As your day so shall your strength be."

— DEUTERONOMY 33:25 ESV

You then decide to make a U-turn, proceed back home, and retrieve your husband's wallet. Why? Because you and your husband are a team. You are a virtuous wife who supports him.

Ladies, your busy life may seem impossible and unbearable some days, but just remember that while you support your husband from behind the scenes, God is uplifting you, sustaining you, encouraging you, and carrying you. Your strength is made perfect in weakness, and He will never give you more than you can bear (I Corinthians 10:13). Now He may send you to heavenly boot camp to build up your spiritual muscles, but know that He has equipped you for the task.

Heavenly Father, I pray for every musician's wife that feels overwhelmed overworked, unappreciated, encumbered with life, and just plain tired. I pray for supernatural strength, well behaved children, remembering husbands, and favor to finish task when it all goes crazy. Remember ladies, God has graced you as the conductor of your family and he that hath begun a good work in you and your family will perform it until the day of Jesus Christ (Philippians 1:6). You Got This.

JESSICA V. WILSON

OUT OF THE SPOTLIGHT

*D*ear First Lady,

I noticed how no one acknowledged you during today's service, and that bothered me. People need to know who you are and applaud you for all the sacrifices you make. But you sit there, not bothered one bit. You cheer on everyone else as recognition is given to everyone but you. You know that all glory belongs to God and feel privileged just to serve without any of the attention.

The husband's role in the life of the first lady should establish a culture for how she should be honored in public. Not only does it bring honor to the marriage and her position in his life, but public appreciation ensures the marriage is distinct and honored above all other relationships. This type of open appreciation sets a boundary around the marriage so that none can violate your position in his life. The law of protection is established to secure the marriage and your position as the first lady.

Here is a story that may help you understand what you need from your husband. A pastor would bring home flowers to his wife, but she seemed un-phased. Out of frustration, he reached out to his sister who gave him great advice. She told him instead of bringing flowers home, have them delivered to her job. What a difference that made. When the wife spoke to the husband, she could not stop blushing.

I am not trying to persuade you to control how your husband appreciates you. Rather, these are words to help you humbly communicate to your husband how important it is for you to feel appreciated as his wife, not just in private, but in public as well. The wife is already under so much scrutiny and judgement in her position. When the first lady is appreciated publicly by her husband, it shows the respect, love, and support that he has for her. How invigorating and refreshing it is to see the pastor admiring his wife and showing affection openly.

Dear pastors' wives, who are feeling ignored, please know that your role in the ministry is also important.

"...he that shall humble himself shall be exalted."

— MATTHEW 23:12 KJV

Dear Lord, I ask that You bless Your servant today. I pray that as she ministers along-side her husband that You would strengthen her. Be the lifter of her head. May everything that she puts her hands to be blessed. Guide her footsteps and protect her from all harm. Remind her to guard her heart and mind with Your peace. Thank You for rewarding her openly for all that she has done for Your glory in secret. We pray these things in Your wonderful, matchless name, Jesus. Amen.

TÁMU MILLER

LONELINESS

*D*ear First Lady,

I understand that one of the biggest challenges of being a wife, mom, and pastor's wife is loneliness. You keep telling yourself that you don't have time to nurture friendships or enjoy any of life's pleasures that were once central to *your* life. Truth is, you didn't make time for those things, and when it was time to reap the rewards, nothing had been sown, leaving you sad and experientially bankrupt.

Loneliness can arise from a multitude of experiences, such as loss of a loved one or the loss of one's identity. When becoming one flesh, it is easy to lose a sense of autonomy, and the added responsibilities of family and ministry take a toll on who we identify ourselves as.

While the children of Israel were on their journey to Canaan, Joshua wanted them to pass over Jordan with the Ark of the Covenant and take stones as commemorative tokens to remind them of God's blessing after crossing the bare floor of the Jordan river, and be able to tell this story to future generations (Joshua 4: 5-6). God wants us to create some mementos for the experiences we are having now—big or small—to celebrate with family. Not just for us, but to pass on the legacy of celebrating the blessing we now have in Christ, instead of what we hope to receive.

Replacing loneliness with the joy of the Lord fills most days with much more love and hope than anything I could have ever imagined. Overcoming this has only been possible through prayer, investing in myself, and commemorating special moments in my life. The voice of the enemy will try to steal your hope and make you feel alone. You are never alone in Christ.

Pray this with me:

Our father God in Heaven, thank You for never leaving or forsaking us. Your faithfulness endures forever. We rejoice in knowing that even we all deserve attention, and we must strive not to forget who You have made us to be and the things we enjoy. Give us discernment so that our time is invested not in distractions, but in experiences that You ordain. In Jesus' name, Amen.

BRANDI OPPENHAMMER

FINDING SAFE PEOPLE

*D*ear First Lady,

Your husband gets the call you've been dreading. His employer is moving to a different state. Just when you've gotten comfortable and have perfected your routine, you have to pick up and move, leaving all that you know and love. After the immediate disappointment fades, you realize that the move is what's best for your family right now. You understand that God has opened this door and promises to always provide. He's done it before and will do it again.

I can remember when we first moved to a new state. It was scary. I had to find a reliable sitter because this Momma wasn't going to leave her children with just anyone. I searched for genuine people. Maybe there was one—a transplant like me—who could understand what I was feeling. Being the social butterfly I am, I wanted someone I could talk to and even have lunch with from time to time. Of course, there's your husband; but I needed some girl-time. Most of us women like to laugh, unwind, trade recipes, and take shopping trips.

Finding safe people, especially in a new space, can be challenging all on its own. You want a friend who you are comfortable comparing notes with to see if you are raising your children the way God says. A friend who holds you accountable for your actions. Someone who will call you out on your mess in love, letting you know, "That ain't right!" while also understanding that you are human, you have feelings, and make mistakes.

It's important to have people in your life that will not talk about you or share your secrets, but will bring you before the Lord in prayer. You know you have a good prayer circle when they will pray for you on the spot without even knowing the details. A friend that's thoughtful, who is just a phone call or text message away with an encouraging word. They have your best interests at heart. They give you godly council and won't steer you wrong.

You will find safe people that may have to move away. At first, you are heart broken and you feel lost, but don't panic. The phone calls and visits will become less frequent, but the trust will become better and stronger. At the same time, God always has a ram in the bush because He never leaves or forsakes us. Your circle begins to grow as another sister-friend is added. These friends are jewels and we must cherish and appreciate them. I thank God for my sister-friends.

> *"A man that hath friends must shew himself friendly: and there is a friend that sticketh closer than a brother."*
>
> — PROVERBS 18:24 KJV

Father God, I want to thank You so very much for covering me and my family. Please continue to guide us in our daily walk. Give us discernment as we meet new people. Provide a safe place and safe people for Your children. Surround us with people that have a heart for You. Help us to show ourselves friendly and love others as You have commanded. In Jesus' name, Amen.

APRIL COLEMAN

8

FEELINGS OF INADEQUACY

*D*ear First Lady,

     For some time now, I attentively observed from afar your quiet, laid-back demeanor not seeking to be up front. But over time I have come to realize those qualities stem from something deeper than a character trait.

You have an awesome responsibility yet you feel overlooked and you make the decision to walk in your husband's shadow. Enveloped in these negative emotions is low self-esteem which eventually takes its toll, leaving you empty, unfulfilled, and spiritually stunted. Rest assure, there are others who can relate to what you are experiencing.

On a personal note, I have always been a relatively quiet person resting in the role as wife and mother. I could say confident in my own skin—or so I thought.

One day after service, the pastor at the time came to me and said, "The Lord told me to have you lead praise and worship." It felt as if someone pulled the rug from under my feet, yet I quickly agreed knowing blessings come with obedience.

The underlining reason for hesitancy derived from being called twiggy and boney as a child, coupled with the daunting fact of having a terrible stuttering problem. Anyone familiar with speech disorders knows one can successfully sing without interruption; still in all honesty, nothing could fully eradicate the feelings of being on display or inadequate.

I eventually learned to compensate for the supposed inadequacies; however, low self-esteem continued to plague and generate fear when singing or speaking before an audience. As time went on, I felt comfortable as a psalmist, often hearing what seemed to be hundreds of angels singing through me.

Several years later, I experienced God's desire to stretch me further. During one of many church shut-ins, everyone was assigned groups according to number. When called upon, one person from each group would expound on a theme.

One evening, a minister asked if I would represent my group. The request posed a significant challenge; but unlike before, there was boldness not previously experienced. Afterwards, I continually rehearsed the sequence of events. It was as if I was watching someone else. The encounter will never be forgotten because it was a catalyst showing me I was called to teach.

Dear Pastors' Wives who feel unnoticed and believe ministry is designed only for your husband. Your husband sets the tone for how others treat you, but eradicating feelings of inadequacy is your responsibility! Make time to self-reflect and realize your journey to freedom will increase your dependency on God. Innate qualities and giftings were put in you for His purpose and will be used not only to help your husband, but the Body of Christ at large.

> "For we are his workmanship, created in Christ Jesus unto
>   good works which God hath before ordained that we should
>   walk in them."
>
> — EPHESIANS 2:10 KJV

Dear Lord, I pray that You will help your servant to seek Your will so that she understands how she jointly fits in the Kingdom. Help her to never under-

estimate her natural talents. I also ask that You help her realize the road to spiritual wholeness requires coming boldly to Your throne to access whatever is needed for the journey. In Jesus' name. Amen.

ELLYN MILLER

9

DON'T GET DISTRACTED

*D*ear First Lady,

Believe God when He tells you that He has a purpose for this plan. Yes, this plan that can be very confusing but somehow God-driven. Daily, you question the church, the people, maybe even the denomination of faith. One day I found myself leaving one denomination to go to another, and not really having the immediate support from friends and family. No one understood the sudden change, not even me.

I was only trying to be obedient. To who exactly? I wasn't sure in the moment. Yet, I would sit in service at my soon-to-be church home, and people-watched and tried to find reasons why God couldn't have wanted me there. To my dismay, I never found it. I didn't have many people to talk to outside of church about the wonderful sermon or the different gifts of the Holy Spirit that I witnessed, because what I was experiencing on this level was unheard of in my previous denomination.

Not many of my friends were on this spiritual journey that God had entrusted me to follow, even though I was feeling spiritually immature. My bible was not my go-to book in time of trouble. Most of the time it was my friends, the same ones that struggled to support this transition God was taking me through. All I had was my obedience to what I hoped was His voice, and the view of God's love every Sunday. I witnessed God's love through my husband, as I watched him lift his hands in adoration to God, as I saw him praise with his lips, and as I saw him consistently bringing his notebook and bible to church to take life application notes. I couldn't ignore what God was doing in my marriage and in my home.

Soon, I would have a husband devoted and committed to serving, which meant sacrifice. That sacrifice would include our Sunday mornings where we would ride with each other and talk about the sermons, and how we felt about my husband attending this 'new' church with me. Would it all be worth it? It would only be a matter of time before this spirit of serving would be birthed in me as well. Could this be a part of God's desire for us to submit to our husbands? Could God be allowing me to see what He means by allowing the man to lead his family? Ephesians 5:22 (NIRV) states, "Wives, follow the lead of your husbands as you follow the Lord." We follow the Lord with ears of obedience, loyalty, and always seeking knowledge, wanting to know how we can serve Him better. Our very own relationship with God is only a guide to our ever-growing relationship with our husband.

Being careful to speak, but quick to learn is very important when God has placed your husband in a leading position because there is so much connected to your bond. God wants us to understand "that the head of every man is Christ, the head of a wife is her husband, and the head of Christ is God" (1 Corinthians 11:3 ESV). Therefore, do not let the noise of others become a distraction that don't understand the spiritual journey God has entrusted you and your husband to follow. Most importantly, do not let your own thoughts become a detour from the birth of new things in your marriage and household.

Dear God, help me die daily to carnal, flesh-led thoughts and desires so that I may seek to only please You with my actions and words. Help me see You in the times that I am unsure of my path during this season while I am trying to live a purpose-filled life. Forgive me for the times that I allowed my own thoughts and my own agenda to get in the way of being used as Your vessel to do Kingdom work. Help me notice opportunities to become more like You and less like the world. Help me to remove the shades of judgment, jeal-

ousy, and deceit so that I may see each one of Your children through Your eyes of love, compassion, and faithfulness. I thank You for never giving up on me, and I will model You so that I will not give up on others. In Jesus name, Amen.

KERI PETTIS

FORGIVENESS AFTER ADULTERY

*D*ear First Lady,

News travels fast. Everybody in the church world knows your business. Here comes the advice... "Support your husband." "Leave him." Questions begin filling your head and now you can't think straight. You're wishing all this was only a dream. But no, this is your reality. You wish the world would stop moving for just a moment so you can get your bearings back. As soon as you think everything is falling apart, you immediately begin to feel the presence and peace of God knowing that He has you in the palm of His hand.

You feel like your future hopes and dreams have been shattered—having children, buying your first home, growing old together. But now you have to decide if you want to stay or leave your husband.

God may tell you to leave, but you may not want to depart. You may want to stay and work things out with your husband, believing that being a loving, supportive wife will fix the problem. As a first lady, your first position is prayer. Seek the will of God concerning your marriage. He will give you a verdict from His throne on His plans to either restore or dissolve your marriage. When He gives you marching orders, be swift to obey Him. You may walk away from your prayer time burdened with one of the hardest decisions you will have to make, but remember, you must still obey God.

So, how could a loving God allow you to go through something so traumatic? God loves you deeply. He will keep you sane through it all. He will hold you up and make you whole. You will experience God in a way that you've never known before. He will fight for you and make you His priority.

Rest assured that God has your back. He is a miracle worker and can turn your situation around. Remember, "...all things work together for good to them that love God" (Romans 8:28a KJV). You still have a purpose. You still have a future.

Forgiveness and healing will happen over a period of time. You'll reach a time when you will no longer be angry about the offense. Believe me. Trust God that it will happen. Be patient. If you need therapy, please go. There are many competent counselors who can help walk you through the process. Adultery can skew your perspective. You may start categorizing all men as cheaters. You may even blame yourself. All manner of thoughts will go through your head, but thank God that He will keep us in perfect peace as we keep our minds on Him because we trust Him (Isaiah 26:3).

> *"The Lord is nigh unto them that are of a broken heart."*
>
> — PSALM 34:18A KJV

> *"For thy Maker is thine husband; the LORD of hosts is his name; and thy Redeemer the Holy One of Israel; The God of the whole earth shall he be called."*
>
> — ISAIAH 54:5 KJV

Father, in the name of Jesus, I come to You right now on behalf of my sister. Oh God, she's hurting right now. But I ask right now that You come to her rescue. Overshadow her with Your wings of protection. Let her know that she is in the palm of Your hand. Let her feel Your presence right now, in the name of Jesus. I rebuke thoughts of giving up on life. I speak into her a renewed mind. I speak into her a peace that surpasses all understanding. I speak into her joy unspeakable and full of glory. God, You are in control and You sit on the throne. You have all power in Your hands. Turn and change her heart toward You. I rebuke any bitterness that may be trying to take root. I ask that You speak to her. Give her direction. Lead her and guide her footsteps. You are an awesome God and we praise You. Greater is He that is in her than he that is in the world. She is more than a conqueror. She is above and not beneath. She is the apple of Your eye. She is Your daughter. You love her with an everlasting love and are near to see about her. Thank You, Lord, for standing up in her. She is Your child and she is royalty. We pray and declare all of these things in Your name, Jesus. Amen. Hallelujah. Be healed, my sister.

TÁMU MILLER

DIVORCE

*H*ey Sis,

So I heard you're going through a divorce. I can empathize and sympathize with you. I went through it as well, and I want you to know that you are not alone in this. I'm here for you. You see, He allowed me to go through this first so that I could be there for you when it was your turn.

I am the divorced one. You know, the one that HAD to have been the reason why the marriage ended in the first place. It was because of my sassy attitude, my smart mouth, my feisty spirit. The one who didn't sing solos, didn't play the piano, and didn't teach the children. The one who was late to church more often than not, nah, just always late. You see, it was never my intention to become the divorced one. Divorce is something you never really predict or plan. Your plan is to grow old together and stay married until "death do you part."

Unfortunately, I was a victim of domestic violence. I suffered in silence for nearly 12 years. I wanted to protect his position in the church, protect his job, and his image with our families. I also wanted to protect my own image because I didn't want to be identified as a weak woman. I thought this was God's way of teaching me forgiveness. I was overwhelmed by fear. Fear that he may want to finish what he started. Fear of being unable to provide for myself and our children. I felt that it was my fault and if I changed my behavior—became less vocal, less opinionated, less sarcastic, less sassy, less feisty—then maybe the abuse would stop. I experienced shame for staying longer than I ever thought I would. I was also embarrassed because my decision to leave was what actually ended my marriage.

> *"Do not be afraid of them, for I am with you and will rescue you," declares the Lord.*
>
> — JEREMIAH 1:8 NIV

> *"When I look back over my life, I see pain, mistakes and heartache. When I look in the mirror, I see strength, learned lessons and pride in myself. It has taken me so long to find my voice and to claim my life as my own."*
>
> — UNKNOWN

I promise you that you will get through this trial as well. What may seem impossible, really is saying, "I'm possible." I AM possible. When you say, "I AM." you are calling on the name of the great I AM. So continue to bring Him forth in your life and presence. Divorce isn't the end of the road or the end of your life. It can actually be the start of something great and fantastic. Allow God the opportunity of giving you exactly what He knows that you deserve.

Dear Jesus, remind me always that You have never given me the spirit of fear. Remind me that Your strength is my strength and Your grace is sufficient. Grow me in Your grace forever. Amen.

LAURRY MANUEL

IT'S NOT THE END

*D*ear First Lady,

How are you today? I happened to be sitting in the foyer when I overheard a young lady sharing how her friends felt she was dressed like a first lady. I quietly listened to her conversation and wondered how much did she really know or understood about the weight of this position. Many young women romanticize the idea of marriage and finding their Prince Charming when they grow older. Sometimes the prince is in ministry, but little do they know that being a first lady is not always about dressing to the nines. There are many days and nights where you and your family are placed on the back burner for the call of ministry. Simply put, many nights are spent alone.

I know that you, as well as many, believe that a lasting relationship will be easy due to the depth of love you have for your husband. Unfortunately, being overlooked continuously weighs upon us and erodes affection for ministry and marriage. Neither does it help the situation any when you are overwhelmed with other demands like having a good job and meeting everyone's expectations. It has been said that we deal with the fish bowl syndrome, where we are always on display for all to see our successes and pitfalls. The demands can create a basket of emotions that are sometimes difficult to process, even with prayer and fasting. I don't know about you, but I have sometimes dealt with anger, depression, defeat, isolation, regret, abandonment, brokenness, and more. I wondered what in the world are we doing here in this relationship and in this ministry. Nothing seems to be working, and I am emotionally worn out. I have taken time off to regroup. I have prayed. I have fasted and read the word. Yet, I still do not feel valued by my husband. His attention seemed to be elsewhere. Where did we fail to fireproof our relationship? Where did we not allow God to work? Where am I to blame? What could I have done differently to keep from being in this place of pain?

First lady, there are some behavioral case studies that show the occurrences of emotional breakdowns and disconnects when a person's basic needs are not met. The physical and emotional part of us has to be satisfied. The fish bowl syndrome, again, does not always allow us to discuss openly the physical and emotional things that we need openly without criticism. It is unfortunate that people place us and our children on a pedestal with expectations that they cannot even live up to themselves. I think people often forget about the Pharisees, the Sadducees, the Law, and the prophets. Jesus told us the greatest commandment is to Love the Lord with All Thine Soul, Heart, and Mind. The second is like unto it in that we need to love our neighbors as ourselves. By walking in Love, we can hang all the law and the prophets (Matt. 22:38-40). Trust me! Loving everyone is not always easy. I was told it was a heart and a faith thing and that I needed to pray and choose love.

We always say that prayer will change things. We have been told time and time again that we need to give it to the Lord and trust Him to handle it. Knowing this to be true, but we still ask, "Does anyone understand what I am going through?" "Does anyone understand that I am tired and I am ready to walk away from this now?" After asking these questions and coming to the point of personal resolve, wrestling with role expectations is still a problem. As the first lady, you are expected to be strong with broad shoulders. You are never supposed to wear the face of pain or express any level of relational discontent. People expect you to keep the home intact by supporting your husband in every facet of ministry. But, what happens when you have completely tapped out of spiritual strength from giving to everyone and doing everything? What happens when your Prince Charming is oblivious to the signs of marital erosion? What happens when they come home and ignore the burden of grief that you shoulder? After all, he is the one that God allowed you to be joined to for life.

I know God provided us a marital roadmap in the Garden of Eden when He created Adam and Eve. Everything that needed to sustain the relationship was already placed in the garden. The spiritual and physical separation did not occur until Eve was tempted, and her appetite was changed after being exposed to something different in her marriage. We also change when we have longings or desires for certain things in our marriage. Our hearts can drift when the expectations are not met or when disappointment occurs. The scriptures give clear examples of marriage. Unfortunately, society has created expectations that conflict with scripture. Moreover, the church has reinforced these imbalanced ideologies of marriage, while furthermore removing God's original design for marriage. The ability to submit becomes difficult when husbands do not fulfill the role as the head or savior of the household.

My prayer today is that every husband will love his wife as Christ loved the church and gave himself for it (Ephesian 5:22-25). I pray that God will strengthen your union and continue to provide and protect your marriage from role imbalances that place pressure upon the relationship. Lord fill any voids in the relationship. As You have allowed this union to occur, Lord we ask that You will allow the husband and wife to function in their purpose or God-given potential. Let them love each other as You love the church and gave yourself for it. Let their love be overflowing with joy unspeakable and full of glory. Let there be no disrespect or usurping of authority. Let each have a listening ear and an ability to discern what is necessary for a romantic, loving, God-centered relationship. Eradicate imbalances, resentments, and emotional disconnects. Restore, rebuild, and regenerate everything that the enemy tries to steal in Jesus' name.

My dear sister, if you are enduring the process of separation/divorce, I warn you that it can be more painful than you realize. You will grieve the loss of status, esteem, identity, community, friends, security, and destiny. This departure will sometimes feel like the end of God's purpose in our lives. This time may also feel like God has forgotten you or does not understand your pain. It may even feel as though all direction is lost. You may even experience a loss of self during that time causing negative thoughts to arise. Allow the scripture to become life in you by meditating on it daily to overcome your pain. Philippians 4:8–9 can help you retrain your thoughts, so that God can be lifted above your circumstances.

> *"Finally, brethren, whatsoever things are true, whatsoever things are honest, whatsoever things are just, whatsoever things are pure, whatsoever things are lovely, whatsoever things are of good report; if there be any virtue, and if there be any praise, think on these things. Those things, which ye have both learned, and received, and heard, and seen in me, do: and the God of peace shall be with you."*
>
> — PHILIPPIANS 4:8–9 KJV

Let me encourage you one last time. Divorce is not the end. God is a restorer. Take the story of Mephibosheth in 2 Samuel chapter 9 as an example of God's restoration. Mephibosheth was the son of a prince, who lost everything as a result of war. His nurse took him to Lo-Debar, a place considered to be a ghetto, where nothing good dwelled. Most certainly, Mephibosheth grieved his position of royalty and all that he lost. Ziba, a servant of King Saul, was summoned by King David. The King inquired, "Is there anyone left from the household of Saul?" The reply: "Yes, Mephibosheth is the son of Johnathan. He is in the house of Machir in Lo-Debar." Long story short, the King sent for him and prepared a place for Mephibosheth at the royal table. On this journey, no doubt, your emotional war causes loss; yet, there is someone familiar with you and your God-given purpose. God will touch. God will move. God will restore your place at the King's table, for you too are royalty.

Lord, we come and ask that You will heal the heart of the first lady. Take away the feelings of disconnect, despair, defeat, grief, abandonment, or anything the enemy would use to attack her emotions. I ask that You will hold her in the palm of Your hands. Keep her under the shadow of Your almighty wings and give her the healing that is necessary to move forward. I need You to forgive us all for our shortcomings. Help us also to forgive and release those who have wronged or offended us. Do not allow us to relish in the past hurts of our marriage. We will not identify with this pain and allow it to rob us of our purpose in You. We will walk in Your goodness. We will rest in Your word. We will honor You with our whole hearts. We believe that everything lost in this process will be restored. We believe that You will restore us to the place of royalty just like You did with Mephibosheth. Help us to rest in You and allow You to carry us through this process. In Jesus' Name. Amen.

SHERLYN WARNER

13

IT WASN'T ME

*D*ear First Lady,

It is with great regret that I must inform you that although you may be innocent as a lamb, the accuser of the brethren is coming for you, your family, your ministry, and your destiny. It is my greatest desire that this letter will strengthen you for your journey. I can honestly tell you that what you have embarked on is not in your control, but you are in the safest place you could ever be and that's in the hands of God. Trust God, your intuition, discernment, the Holy Ghost, and the Word only. Prayer is a must for this journey.

> *"In return for my love they are my accusers, But I give myself to prayer."*

— PSALMS 109:4 NKJV

I was accused of having an inappropriate relationship with a female member of my church by someone who I thought was my friend.

"Liar!" Anger began to rise from the depths of my soul. How was I supposed to look at her without anger? How could I talk to her like nothing ever happened?

The old me would have cursed her out. The old me would have sucker punched her at our next encounter. But the new me could not do that at all. The new me was sanctified and filled with the Holy Ghost. The new me had to pray for the one that despitefully betrayed me. The new me had to do it for the good of the ministry by taking another one for the team. You see, you must not compromise the Holy Ghost's progress in you since salvation. The adversary was after my character, my witness, and my peace. I wasn't giving up without a fight. A Holy Ghost fight.

There is no first lady's manual that prepares you for this. I had no mentor. I could not talk to anyone in the church about the situation. Neither could I vent to my mom, friend, or family members. You see, as a first lady you must protect your child. I know you are saying, "What child?" The church. The gift God has given us comes with a great price. Ready or not, you have been called and chosen. You can never fully count the costs that this position will require of you. What you need to be sure about is you are responsible for the gift God has given you. Protect it like you would protect your child. Your ministry is precious. Your gift and calling are precious. You are precious and the apple of our Heavenly Father's eye.

You see, when the enemy raises his ugly head you must do what Jesus would do. You cannot wrestle against the flesh of the betrayer. You may want their blood, their marriage, their peace to be disturbed like yours may have been, but nevertheless God is your present help in your time of trouble.

We are always learning through every experience. You are stretched, strengthened, and established with every test. One day, I walked into church and realized I was free from anger and pain. Time, prayer, worship, the word, and God had worked on my behalf. I was healed. Hallelujah!

God has and will always keep you, if you want to be kept.

As a first lady, you may not hear all the details, lies, or betrayals, but what you must do is stay the course.

Therefore, my beloved brethren, be steadfast, immovable,
always abounding in the work of the Lord, knowing that
your labor is not in vain in the Lord.

— 1 CORINTHIANS 15:58 NKJV

Lord Abba, Almighty Father God, bless my sister in Christ to overcome every obstacle that tries to dismantle her from her position. Give her power, love, and a sound mind. Give her wisdom and freedom. Protect her marriage, children, ministry, and victories in Jesus name. Make her steadfast, immoveable, and always bounding in the work of the LORD. Let prayer, worship, and the word always be her weapons of choice in Jesus name. Amen.

KRYSTAL HENRY

14

HUSH

*D*ear First Lady,

Another late night. You were sleep before he made it home, and you only have brief moments in the morning before he's headed out the door again. Business needs to be handled and it doesn't seem like there are enough hours in the day. Frustration sets in. You need more time. You need him to help with the children so you can take a break. But just when you begin to open your mouth or make a phone call to release your frustrations, the Lord whispers, "Hush."

Sound familiar? I've found myself in this situation many times. Every time I would want to call and ask, "Where are you?" or "When are you coming home?", I would hear the Lord say to me gently, "Hush. Don't call." Most of the time, if not all of the time, I knew exactly where my husband was and what he was doing. I just wanted him to hurry along and get home. I had to realize that my husband was not spending hours away because he didn't want to be around me. He is a ministry leader and is called to serve. He was just doing the work of the Lord.

I remember my husband playing the drums for a church we attended. It was at a Wednesday night bible class, and service had just dismissed. The hour was late. I had to be at work the next morning and was growing irritated of the wait. But there my husband was, playing the drums with other musicians in an after-church jam session. Needless to say, I was ready to go.

While standing in the back of the church, I gave my husband "the eye" and, to my regret, the other musicians saw me. After my husband and the other musicians finished playing, he walked over to me and said, "Don't you ever do that again. I'm serving as the drummer tonight, and I need for you to wait." After I got over the "how-dare-you-talk-to-me-that-way" stare, I realized that I owed him an apology. That episode showed me how much working in his ministry-gift meant to him. He did not take it lightly. This is now something I truly admire about him. His work ethic in the secular and spiritual arenas is impeccable. I never want to be a hindrance to what God is doing in his life.

Over the years, we've understood that there has to be balance in our marriage. Communication is so important to understand what to expect and what is to be expected. Your marriage will go through different seasons. What you may have required at one time may be different for you now. Communication. Communication. Communication. You can't go wrong with this, and you certainly can't over-do it.

My husband is still called on quite a bit to serve, and I totally support him. What's truly a blessing is that he knows when he needs to slow down and spend quality time with his family. In the process, I've gotten out my comfort zone and started doing things that I'm passionate about. There's a number of activities you can participate in or join, such as taking a class and/or becoming a volunteer. One of the greatest benefits of getting involved is that you will broaden your knowledge and conversation with your spouse. How awesome it will be to talk about more than just ministry, kids, and bills. Imagine you and your husband reaching a whole other level of intimacy.

> "Nevertheless let every one of you in particular so love his wife even as himself; and the wife see that she reverence her husband."

> — EPHESIANS 5:33 KJV

Lord, thank You for this virtuous woman. I pray that she continues to hear Your voice clearly and obeys. Let her be a woman that builds up her house and not tear it down. As she speaks to her husband, let her words be seasoned and laced with love. Teach her and her husband how to effectively communicate and respect one another. Show them how to serve one another and be what the other one needs. In Jesus' name, Amen.

TÁMU MILLER

15

IT'S A PRINCIPALITY THING

*H*ello, First Lady,
        I send you this letter of endurance to encourage your hearts, to look beyond what the flesh sees and perceive all matters with the heart of God. I also send you this letter so that you might see who you are in the Spirit and to understand your God-given purpose.

> *"And the Lord God said, it is not good that the man should be alone; I will make him an help meet for him."*
>
> — *GENESIS 2:18 KJV*

...an help meet...

In 1998, I married a single dad, the minister of music and a B.K. (Bishop's kid). In doing so, we endured a host of issues—jealousy and hatred from women in the church and manipulation by so called friends trying to destroy us from within by putting our girls against each other. Unresolved issues and baggage from our previous marriages also played a part in the underlying frustration of our marriage. I won't go into detail about the things we had to endure in our marriage. I'll save that for another book! But after being married for 20 years, I have come into the knowledge of who I am and my purpose. That also includes who my husband is and his purpose. Not in title, but who God called us to be.

I stated the later verse of Genesis 2:18 *"help meet"* because this speaks to our purpose set by God. God clearly showed me that I am to help my husband meet the goals He has set for him. I'm not just talking about the domestic side of the marriage—cooking, cleaning, managing the home, and taking care of the children and his need—but taking care of the spiritual needs as well.

We are the intercessors. We must pray for the overall success of the family, which includes the children, the business, the marriage, and the ministry. You must be keen about these areas going into the relationship because the enemy knows the threat you are to his kingdom. And if you both know who you are, and you are walking in your purpose, then together you are an unstoppable force for the Kingdom of Heaven.

Your marriage being an unstoppable force for God's Kingdom is why Satan sends the attacks from the women with a Jezebel and Delilah spirit. That`s why He sends you into a head trip when your husband is late coming home and you start thinking he's with that woman that kissed him on the cheek Sunday. No.

Stop looking at what's happening through the eyes of the flesh and start looking at it in the spirit. Bind those thoughts with the Word of God.

It`s a Principality thing.

> *"Casting down imaginations, and every high thing that*
> *exalteth itself against the knowledge of God, and bringing*
> *into captivity every thought to the obedience of Christ; And*
> *having in a readiness to revenge all disobedience, when*
> *your obedience is fulfilled.*
>
> — 2 CORINTHIANS 10:5, 6 KJV

We have to get in the fight with Him. Completely cover your husband in prayer day and night because of the mandate set upon him by the Lord. Our husbands are, and will be, attacked from every angle; therefore, we can't be distracted by silly women or men in the church. Handle the situation in a godly way and don't let it be your focus. Spend time praying in tongues. This will help you get stronger in your spiritual communication with God. And if you are a dreamer, journal your dreams and your prayers. That way, you will always know the fight that is before you. You have work to do.

> *"For we wrestle not against flesh and blood but against principalities..."*

> — EPHESIANS 6:12 KJV

If I had fully understood this scripture 10 years ago like I understand it now, I would have been spared the emotional trauma that comes with being married in ministry.

In a marriage, the character of the husband and wife will be different, but together we balance. When you are balanced and walking together in ministry, you become a mighty weapon in God's hand.

Father, my prayer for your beautiful daughter is that she seeks wisdom at this time in her life and that she walks in all that You called her to be. I ask that she be strengthened with power to stand against every attack that she may face along her journey. Open her eyes to see the enemy's plan afar off and give her strategies to overthrow them. Guide her feet and help her succeed in every area of her life. Let her see herself as You see her. Show her how to put up a defense wall of prayer through scripture; to protect her marriage, children, business, and ministry! In Jesus' name. Amen.

SHAWANA L. FOSTER

LOVE YOUR NEIGHBOR AS YOURSELF

*D*ear First Lady,

We oftentimes make commitments that seemingly make us happy. However, I have come to discover that most engagements we accept overwhelms our schedules, leaving us feeling exhausted soon after the event. This type of living keeps us from fulfilling our purpose and from obeying God's Command, to love one another as we love ourselves. Let's face it, as pastors' wives we are oftentimes overly committed exhausted, irritable, and unloving.

I can recall being extremely exhausted after a full week of activities, not to mention a long day of work. I was involved in commitments that seemed as if they were beneficial, but they were keeping me from fulfilling my purpose and causing me to be very cantankerous towards my husband and children. As I mentioned before, my life was full of activities and commitments, and even though I was serving in ministry at my church along with my husband, I was oftentimes involved in too many church engagements, and I was not giving enough love to myself and others.

I did my best to go the extra mile and wanted to be the best for everyone, but I was stretched frightfully thin. For instance, I was involved in church activities that took much of my time after work, in addition, I was involved in my children's football, volleyball, basketball, and cheer squad practices and games. I also attended technology and reading camps with them and assisted them with homework assignments and school projects as well. I even volunteered at their school, attended special events, and meetings.

Although I smiled and found a great way to outwardly hold it all together, I was honestly beginning to wear myself thin.

After some thought and quiet time with God during a morning prayer, I realized I was not providing my family and friends with something they needed most, something that Jesus Christ demonstrated on the cross and something that God commanded me to do. It was love for myself and for others. I was not demonstrating the love that Paul clearly defines in 1 Corinthians 13:8, though I was involved in all of these things that seemed meaningful.

For this reason, I put my list of things to do away and everything I thought I had to have my hands in. I continued to pray and asked God to give me the power to love my neighbor as I love myself and to help me better fulfill my purpose and to better obey his commandments.

> "*And you shall love the Lord your God with all your heart and with all your soul and with all your mind and with all your strength.' The second is this: 'You shall love your neighbor as yourself.' There is no other commandment greater than these.*"
>
> — MARK 12:30-31 ESV

Dear Lord, thank You for Your grace, Your mercy, and for Your forgiveness. Thank You for demonstrating unconditional love toward us and thank You for loving us while we were yet sinners.

Jesus, thank You for dying on the cross for our sins and for allowing us to be a part of Your family. Thank You, Lord, that we are set apart for Your glory.

Lord help us to demonstrate unconditional love toward our family and toward others. Help us to do more loving gestures to please You. Help us to practice unconditional love daily. In the name of our Savior Jesus Christ. Amen.

SCHERRIE JONES

EXPERIENCE IS A TEACHER

*D*ear First Lady,

I watched you as you walked to your seat. You looked awkward and uncomfortable. Thoughts may have been running through your mind such as, *Was my husband really called? Am I capable of doing this? How can we lead these people? I feel so out of place.* But there you were, still standing tall through all your uncertainty. Instead of being fixated on your uncertainty, you choose to focus on the gospel that delivers and sets people free. You understand that the ministry is not about you, but it's about Jesus Christ.

Being in this role can be an adjustment, especially if you don't consider yourself social among other things. You'll need to love people who come from all walks of life, not just those who are familiar. God will send experiences your way so that you get to that place. This will be an ongoing process. Nobody is perfect, but God will perfect you in this role.

Be patient and try not to be so hard on yourself through the grooming process. Don't doubt that you and your husband have been called for such a time as this. Your ministry is unique and will draw certain types of people. Where your church and ministry are planted is all ordained by God Himself.

In the beginning stages of building up your ministry, do not change your personality or the core of who God created you to be. Be yourself. A lot of time, effort, perseverance, finances, and energy go into building up a new ministry. Don't lose yourself over time, while wearing the many hats you will have to put on. Most importantly, don't lose your ear to the Lord on what He's called you to do. You'll have to juggle taking care of family, church, and yourself. Don't let anyone force you into doing something that you were not called to do. Don't allow people to put responsibilities on you that make you feel uncomfortable. Just because you are the first lady doesn't mean you have to be the speaker at every women's luncheon. You may be more suited for assisting others with décor and menu planning for special events.

Now when it comes to responsibilities, I am not speaking about turning down obligations because you don't feel like supporting that day. There are times where you may feel this way, but continue to be the loving wife who is always supportive of her husband. Continue to be extremely wise and prayerful about every decision you make.

> "Being confident of this very thing, that he which hath begun a good work in you will perform it until the day of Jesus Christ."

> — PHILIPPIANS 1:6 KJV

Lord, thank You for building my sister's confidence in You by performing Your Word in her life and bringing every promise to pass. I thank You that she can rely on You for reassurance and strength through this season in her life. You will finish the work You have started and oh what a beautiful masterpiece You have created her to be. I thank You for giving her peace as she keeps her mind on You and for clarity in the direction You will have her to go. In Jesus' name, Amen.

TÁMU MILLER

INVISIBLE

*D*ear First Lady,

I see you. You are so strong and so sweet. Sometimes I watch people approach you and pastor and brush past you without the slightest nod that you are even visible.

Other times they sneer, look you up and down, and then force out a hello, I guess because they don't want to be rude and "not speak".

I really know you are saved, saved, because if that was me, I am not sure what I would do. I know in Genesis the Bible says we are made in the image of God, but for some reason people think that excludes you. I know you have heard it all, "Why did he marry her?" and "They don't match." All the way to, "It must be the cook, cause it ain't the looks."

I, for one, think you are beautiful. I know what it is like to fall in love with a person and not their title. I am so glad you have loved God enough, loved yourself enough, and loved pastor enough to endure the side glances, slights, and shuns.

One time though, I saw it got to you. The church was celebrating the Pastoral Anniversary. Twenty years! I know it flew by. They bought y'all a vacation to Hawaii. That gift was so amazing, but they didn't stop there. They presented pastor with multiple gifts and cash love offerings from each auxiliary, and then at the end of all the special presentations, they thanked you as an afterthought for standing by his side.

I watched as presenter after presenter gave him their gifts and none acknowledged you or said, "This is for both of you." That day, I knew that I should pray for you. I actually played a part in it all. It wasn't until I saw your face, ever so gently fall into a frown that I noticed the hurt and neglect. You caught it quickly, but not quick enough. I just want you to know I am sorry, and I see you. More importantly, God sees you and great will be your reward for your service to Him, your husband, your family, and the congregation.

"Rejoice ye in that day, and leap for joy: for, behold, your reward is great in heaven: for in the like manner did their fathers unto the prophets."

— LUKE 6:23 KJV

Lord, may You give Your daughter patience as she continues to serve You with grace and grit, in Jesus' name, Amen.

ARPIL D. BARKER

19

LEADING WHILE BLEEDING

*D*ear First Lady,

It saddened me to see how some of the church members disrespected or insulted you on more than one occasion. The deliberate mispronouncing of your name, an item or person sitting in your designated chair, your picture cropped out of a photo of you and your husband, and being invited to the same functions as your husband's ex-wife who is on program, just to name a few. Please know that the strength and resilience you exude is admired as you so gracefully stand in the confidence of knowing who you are.

Major trauma in the body of Christ can cause "internal bleeding". Symptoms in the natural body causes low blood pressure, abnormal heartbeat, and bruising. However, in the spiritual realm it can cause a decrease in joy, love, and participation.

During the process, you can become discouraged and decline requests to minister when you are truly needed. And yes, you are needed. You have been called to that church and congregation. You are on an assignment. God has built you for this and will give grace to fulfil His purpose in your life, which is why the "internal bleeding" must stop as soon as possible before another vital area of the body is affected.

In the natural, R.I.C.E. is the treatment for recovery—Rest, Ice, Compression, Elevation. However, the spirit requires a different diagnosis.

> "Recompense to no man evil for evil. Provide things honest in
>   the sight of all men."
>
> — ROMANS 12:17 KJV

> "I lead in the way of righteousness, in the midst of the paths of
>   judgment."
>
> — PROVERBS 8:20 KJV

> "The Lord is gracious, and full of Compassion; slow to anger,
>   and of great mercy."
>
> — PSALM 145:8 KJV

> "May the God who gives Endurance and who supplies
>   Encouragement grant that you be of the same mind with
>   one another according to Christ Jesus."
>
> — ROMANS 15:5 AMP

My dear First Lady, the cause, symptoms, diagnosis, and treatment has come to establish you in the sight of the Lord, your husband, and the church. Your position is high profile and you are being watched. So let your recovery be swift, graceful, and pleasing unto the Lord. Your love for ministry will return to you in full measure.

Lord, I ask You to strengthen the heart of Your daughter. She has answered yes to the call and is eager to serve You.

I ask that You guard her heart and mind with Your peace. Use her as a conduit of Your love. As she pours out and minsters, refill, revive, replenish, and restore her.

Heal any hurt like only You can and let forgiveness flow from her heart.

Continue to order her steps. Continue to fight for her. For You, oh Lord, are her shield and the lifter of her head. In Jesus' name. Amen.

DAUGHTER OF JUDAH

20

REDEMPTION: RECOVERY AFTER A "FAILED" MINISTRY

*D*ear First Lady,
   I know it was embarrassing when you and your husband had to close the doors of your ministry. The thought of starting over again is overwhelming. "What will people say? Where do we go from here?" You know looking to God for direction on your next steps is critical. You stand together in strength knowing God will not steer you wrong.

Failed is defined as something or someone not functioning properly; broken-down. Failure is the state or condition of not meeting a desirable or intended objective, and *may* be viewed as the opposite of success. Questions you and your husband should ponder:

1. DID YOU VENTURE THE WAY THE LORD INSTRUCTED?

God said to go ahead and purchase a building, but you wanted to play it safe and start your ministry in your home. God told you to find a building in a particular area, but it looked a bit too rough for you. Maybe God told you to hold off from signing a lease because He didn't want you to get tied into a shoddy deal where you could not handle the mortgage. You have to step out in faith. If God said to move, believe that He has all provision in place to make it happen.

2. DO YOU NEED TO TAKE A BREAK?

God is telling you to take care of a personal issue, but you feel like it's not the right time. You are in your prime and feel like you will lose your current following. You are not realizing how that issue is seeping out of you onto others. Sit down. Get the help that you need. How great will it be to share your testimony and process to victory? The anointing on your life will be stronger than before. You will be able to truly say that you know God as a deliverer because of your experience.

"Let your light so shine before men, that they may see your good works, and glorify your Father which is in heaven."

— MATTHEW 5:16 KJV

3. DID YOU MOVE TOO SOON, TOO FAST?

You didn't follow proper protocol through leadership because you were too anxious. Yes, you were called but things have to be done decently and in order. Don't rush the process. David was anointed King but still went back to shepherding. There was more training God required. We must be patient. We must be sensitive to the Holy Spirit and movement of God. Please know that a loving leader will not hinder what God is doing in your life. They want to see you launch out and do even greater things. They will be cheering you on and providing guidance along the way for a lifetime. First lady, did you put some pressure on your husband? Most often, we see the potential in our husbands before they can. Or maybe they are aware, but fearful. I know this can be frustrating, but take the time to pray that your husband's character and stamina are built and that his love for God grows tremendously. Encourage him and watch how God moves in his life. Trust that God is preparing your husband. No time is wasted.

Was or is it truly a failure, or is God transitioning you? Is God saying to go a different way or use a different approach? Don't allow this encounter to break you. That's exactly what this is: an encounter with the Most-High God. Do not let depression take root. God always finishes what He starts. You are special to Him and He wants to use you. Do you not realize the impact you've already made and how many have given their lives to Christ through your ministry?

Delay is not denial. Remember that you were called. Nothing and no one can change that. God's word does not return to Him void, and it will accomplish what it was sent out to do. You can testify that God can help you to recover all that you have lost because He's done it for you. God can make your name great again.

Go ahead. Reset and regroup.

> "For as the rain cometh down, and the snow from heaven, and returneth not thither, but watereth the earth, and maketh it bring forth and bud, that it may give seed to the sower, and bread to the eater: So shall my word be that goeth forth out of my mouth: it shall not return unto me void, but it shall accomplish that which I please, and it shall prosper in the thing whereto I sent it."
>
> — ISAIAH 55:10, 11 KJV

> "And let us not be weary in well doing: for in due season we shall reap, if we faint not."
>
> — GALATIANS 6:9 KJV

Dear Lord, this is one hard pill to swallow, but I know that You are not a God of confusion. You are a lamp unto our feet and a light unto our path. Our steps have been ordered from the foundation of the world. You knew this day was coming and You also know what my future holds. I'm so glad You are Alpha and Omega, the beginning and the ending. You are the author and finisher of our faith.

Thank You, Lord, for allowing me to make a comeback from my setbacks. I am moving forward. I am pressing forward. You love me enough to put me on a straight path.

You love me so much that You are making sure that I align with Your perfect will. No, this season is not the easiest thing to go through, but I know that I can do all things because You give me the strength. In Jesus' name. Amen.

TÁMU MILLER

21

HEALED BY HIS WORD

*D*ear First Lady,

Sickness, affliction, infirmity, and disease can wreak havoc, physically and mentally, on an individual. I know that you can identify with the physical, mental, and emotional tolls sickness can take on your life. You've endured doctor visit after doctor visit, surgery after surgery, procedure after procedure. Sometimes you feel so alone and question, "Does my spouse still love me? Do my children and/or the congregants view me as weak? Is God angry with me due to unconfessed sin from my past?" It seems you have gotten more than your share of the effects of Adam and Eve's disobedience in the Garden of Eden.

While God does not cause sickness, affliction, infirmity, or disease, He can use them all for His glory. One day, while seeking God for direction during a time of intense sickness in my life, I was given a mandate. I then questioned, "How can I do this, Lord, if I am in pain, fatigued, and nauseous?" He emphatically replied, "I will heal you as you go." I have held onto His word for four years now and He has been true to His word. I have witnessed His healing power as I continue to do what He commands in every season of my life.

To every first lady experiencing sickness, affliction, infirmity, or disease, you have blessed assurance that HE is the Great Physician capable of sending His word to heal you. The scripture emphatically declares:

> *"He sent His word and healed them and delivered them from*
> *their destructions."*

> — PSALM 107:20 KJV

Before going to the Cross of Calvary, Jesus took 39 stripes to conquer the 39 major causes of every sickness and disease in the earth. In Luke 17:14 (ESV), Jesus gave the lepers a mandate. As they obeyed Him, the Bible says, "that as they went they were cleansed."

First lady, your condition is not your conclusion. Through prayer, faith, and His Word, you too will be healed as you obey what He commands in this season of your life.

Thank you, Lord, for allowing me to be a living, breathing, walking testimony of Your healing virtue and power. As my healing manifests, may others witness Your Glory and give You the praise. In Jesus' name. Amen.

Healing is what God does; health is what we do.

ANDREA L. THOMAS

22

HELLO BEAUTIFUL!

*D*ear First Lady,

      At times, we can be our worst critic. Thinking and saying things to ourselves like, *No, not another stretch mark. I should have used more Shea Butter and Vitamin E Oil on my skin during this last pregnancy. My breasts are flat and saggy. I nursed so long and now my breast have disappeared. I need some implants or a least a great bra. I looked horrible in that dress on Sunday. Who asked Mrs. Johnson to post that picture on social media? I need to get it together.* My dear sister, please remember that you are unique. There is not another person like you. God created you and *saw everything that he had made, and, behold, it was very good.*

Oftentimes, as women called by God, we struggle with finding good things to say about ourselves. We are professionals, moms, pastors' wives, and leaders in the church, yet we still struggle with insecurities and self-confidence. We struggle with our image and are overly concerned with our appearance and what others think. I would receive compliments on my hair, makeup, and even how great I looked in my little black dress after giving birth to four children, but because of my insecurities, I struggled with accepting those compliments.

Our insecurities will even cause us to place blame on others. I remember getting angry at my husband and accusing him of not complimenting me on specific things. I felt he was not being thought-ful. He graciously offered me a nice compliment and began sharing with me that it was time to move past my insecurities because they were impeding me from achieving God's best for me. He reminded me that I was beautiful and made in God's image. I was chosen by God and I was called to lead with confidence. His words strongly gripped my heart and I was convicted.

The next morning, I decided that it was time to do something about my insecurities. I decided to go on a fast for seven days and spend inti-mate time with God and focus on His word concerning my value. You, as well, may need to take some time in consecration. Pray and share your concerns with God. Most importantly, ask God to assist you with being completely good with yourself and to feel confident with being beautifully and wonderfully made by Him. In addition, ask God to do something special on the inside by removing the insecurities so that you can live out your purpose and enjoy His best.

I had made a decision and you can too. Look in the mirror and recite these words, "Hello Beautiful."

> *"I will praise thee; for I am fearfully and wonderfully made:*
> *marvelous are thy works; and that my soul knoweth right*
> *well. How precious also are thy thoughts unto me, O God!*
> *How great is the sum of them!"*
>
> — PSALM 139:14, 17 KJV

Dear Lord, You are merciful, gracious, Holy, and blameless. You never make a mistake. You have created us in Your image, and we are wonderful because of You. Lord, thank You for redeeming us and for saving us from the penalty of sin. We belong to You and we are a beautiful part of Your creation. Thank You for creating us. Thank You for valuing us, for seeing beautiful and wonderful things in us. In the name of our Savior Jesus Christ. Amen.

SCHERRIE JONES

ABOUT THE CONTRIBUTORS

ANDREA L. THOMAS

Andrea L. Thomas was born in St. Louis, Missouri in June 1965 to the late Ivory Perry, Jr. and the late Anna Belle Cox-Perry, who were heavily involved in the Civil Rights Movement of the 1960s. A book was written in 1988 about her dad's life and experiences entitled: "A Life in the Struggle: Ivory Perry and the Culture of Opposition". This book is required reading in African-American Studies at various Colleges and Universities throughout the United States.

Andrea was united in marriage to Prophet Dwayne Thomas on August 5, 1995, who has faithfully supported her in ministry. In July 2000, they were blessed with their first and only child, a daughter, Essence Marie.

It is Andrea's desire to do the will of her Heavenly Father by seeing that lost souls are saved and delivered, and the Body of Christ healthy and whole. In May 2002, Andrea received a bachelor's degree in Christian Education from the Sacramento Theological Seminary and Bible College.

In 2013, Andrea retired from the State of California with over twenty years of experience in Supervision, Education and Training. She and her husband, Dwayne, were the founders and pastors of

Another Dimension Apostolic Ministries (A.D.A.M.) in Elk Grove, California where they pastored for ten years. In 2014, God shifted their ministry to that of prophetic evangelists. In 2014, Andrea founded and launched Precise Impact Network (P.I.N.): An Apostolic/Prophetic Motivational Ministry as well as a women's internet mentoring ministry called Diamond Princess E-Mentoring Group (DPEG).

Andrea's vision and mission in this season of her life is "Bringing Kingdom Credibility to the Lives of Believers" and "Motivating People to Pinpoint God's Will and Purpose for their Lives" by preaching the Acceptable Year of the Lord!

ઠ

To my mother, the late Evangelist Anna Belle Cox: Thank you for raising me and my siblings in the fear and the admonition of the Lord. I appreciate the wisdom you instilled in us through your personal testimonies and through the Word of God. For the past 19 years, you've been asleep in Jesus yet your life continues to speak volumes through your children and grandchildren. Thank you for being my mother, my mentor, and my friend.

To my husband, Dwayne Mitchell Thomas: Thank you for being a true man of God. Many times, you pushed me toward my passions and allowed me to burn the candle at both ends of the stick. For this I am grateful. You have been nothing less than supportive throughout our 23-year marriage. Thank you for encouraging me in times when I felt I could not accomplish the task before me. You mean the world to your "best girls" (me and our daughter, Essence). Thank you for being my Boaz Boo.

To my daughter, Essence Marie Thomas: You have been such a blessing to your dad and me. Thank you for understanding during times when I had to put down my "Mom Hat" to do other things. It is a joy watching you grow both in the natural and in the Spirit into the young woman God has called you to be. Thank you for allowing me to act silly with you. Your encouragement propels me forward.

To my friend and the visionary of this devotional book project,

Támu Miller: Thank you, Támu, for hearing the Holy Spirit and asking me to be a part of this great project. It took great courage for you to address pastors' wives (first ladies) and the issues they face and often suffer in silence. God's continuous blessings upon every dream and vision you conceive and birth for His Kingdom purpose.

APRIL DISHON BARKER

April Dishon Barker is the CEO and Founder of Empire of Dreams, LLC where she develops dream-building plans with people in high-level leadership to help bring their ideas from mental to manifestation. Her first dream-building project is building a beautiful life with her husband of 17 years, Marco, and their four children whom she serves wholeheartedly with great joy. She also is a licensed minister and published author. She is committed with abandon to a life of service to her Lord and Savior Jesus Christ. April's God-given mission is to "Proclaim God's Word through Psalms, Prayer, Pen, Preaching, and Prophecy". Her lifestyle of worship comes from pure gratitude for the work of Calvary.

Thanks to Mrs. Támu Miller for this opportunity.

Dedicated to all my brothers in the Body of Christ who serve in their local churches faithfully.

APRIL COLEMAN

April Coleman is a hairdresser, wife, and mother from Dallas, Texas who has been married for 19 years. Her husband and she moved from Texas to Emporia, Kansas where they lived for a two-and-a-half-year pit stop. From there they moved to Sioux City, Iowa where they have lived for a little over ten years. It has been a roller coaster ride and she would definitely take it over and over again.

First, I want to thank Mrs. Támu Miller for considering me to participate in this devotional. It has been an experience, I tell you. Second, my family, my husband, Clifton, love you dearly, baby. Thank you for your support. My daughters, Autumn and Courtney, for giving Mommy space to write. All of my Sioux City sister's in Christ.

This is dedicated to all the hard-working women, wives, and mothers praying and supporting our men and families. Keep up the good work, it's paying off. Also, to my daughters, always put God first. May your dreams come true. Be real and true to yourself and others.

BRANDI OPPENHAMMER

Brandi Oppenhammer is a veteran educator whose career has included teaching secondary science and creating training and development content for an industry-leading insurance marketplace in the North Texas area. She and her family currently attend Lifeway Church of Dallas and lead an exciting youth ministry and security team. As an experienced training specialist, she has dedicated her career to connecting people with their passion and strengths team building. A graduate of Paul Quinn College, her undergraduate tenure included college choir, student leadership, pan-hellenic association, and Miss Paul Quinn 2001-2002, an honor which would be documented both locally and nationally. Her greatest accomplishment, however, is being a mother to Brea, Jasmine, Jalen, and Brooklyn, and wife to Johnny Oppenhammer.

My name is Mrs. Brandi Oppenhammer, and the topic closest to my heart personally was dealing with loneliness. As an educator, wife, mother, and first lady, it was important to me to acknowledge a reality that many of us on a similar path experience.

છે.

I would like to thank Támu Miller, a young lady I have known for nearly 20 years, that is a visionary and a woman after God's heart. Thank you for your obedience, patience, passion, and including me on this project. I would also like to thank my family, my husband primarily, for being an encourager to do the best things. He has been my confidant, pastor, and friend for 14 years and my personal growth with God was more important to him than even to myself at times, I think. To my very first teacher, Dr. Helen Jackson, who was the best image of a mother and grandmother, and who is the embodiment of selfless love and dedication to her children and family. This devotional will be dedicated to her and my family for believing in me to fulfill my potential. To my children, I love you and God has a bounty of blessings waiting to reward your hard work and obedience to him. Find your passion and use God's gifts for his glory. To my husband, I thank God for your obedience, and your love, and I can't wait to see how he blesses your ministry in leading men to God.

CARLA HAMILTON

Carla Hamilton is a credentialed elementary school teacher. She is dedicated to loving and serving in her community and at Spirit and Life Ministries in San Fernando Valley. Carla is married to Bishop Stephen Hamilton and has two children, Angela and Randall. She earned her bachelor's degree from UCLA and enjoys reading and traveling.

Dedicated to Bishop Hamilton, Angela, Randall, Minnie, Thelma, Bernita, and Richard.

DAUGHTER OF JUDAH

I am a wife, mother, and grandmother absolutely loving my life. I bow before Christ free to serve Him in peace. I have worked in banking and other financial markets for many years. I am glad to be a part of this book project.

ELLYN MILLER

Ellyn Miller serves her local church in several capacities and has a long administrative career in higher education. She finds it rewarding helping high school and college students reach their aspirations. The desire to obtain a college degree was postponed so that she could focus attention on nurturing and training her children.

While lending her talents to assisting non-profits, after 24 years, Ellyn completed lifelong desire by returning to school. Education includes a Bachelor of Science in Organizational Leadership and Master of Arts in Human Resource Management, Specialization in Organizational Leadership. Married 37 years, Ellyn has five children, two daughters-in-love, one son-in-love, and 11 grandchildren.

❧

My deepest gratitude to God. You continue to be my source and strength. Life is a journey that should not be taken without You.

A special thank you to my family. We are doing life together to fulfill God's purpose. The best is yet to come!

To my church family, thank you for being patient as I blossom into being a mature gift to the body of Christ.

JESSICA WILSON

I am the Branch Chief, Acquisition Directorate, Foreign Military Sales with the United States Coast Guard and Business Owner Extraordinaire at "AskJessEventsllc". My greatest accomplishments in life are my walk with Christ, my wonderful husband, Corey, of 10 years, my handsome sons, London and Langston, and my amazing career spanning fifteen years, traveling coast to coast. God has truly been good to me, and for that I am grateful.

§

I am immensely honored and humbled in being a part of this devotional project. Támu, thank you for being a source of inspiration, motivation, and encouragement. To every first lady, minister's wife, musician's wife, deacon's wife, and leading lady who supports their husbands tirelessly, I Honor You! Words alone are inadequate in offering my thanks to those women who stand alongside their spouses. Your encouragement and cooperation in "Project Managing" your family and home is simply amazing. Finally, I would like to express my sincere thanks to God, my husband, my amazing sons, and a beloved network of Indestructibly Strong, Beautiful, Virtuous Leading Ladies. I love you all!

KERI PETTIS

Keri Pettis is a mother, wife, educator, and a lover of Christ. She currently works as a Youth & Children Specialist at Buckner International, where she can spread not only tangible love but Biblical love by caring for God's children. She attended Oakwood University, where she graduated in 2010 with a Bachelor's in Healthcare Administration and a minor in Marketing. Soon after, she married the love of her life, Andrew Pettis, and together they care for their son, Esrel. She returned to school while working in the medical field and obtained her Master's in Public Administration and was certified in Non-Profit Management. She loves to serve others and sees it as another form of worship. She currently serves in two youth ministries at her local church and finds joy in watching kids learn about the love of Jesus. If you want to engage in conversation with her, just start talking about the goodness of God and she is sold. Her love for Christ permeates in her home life, work life, and most importantly with the women she interacts with daily. Keri has an empowering ministry for women named She Fights She Wins, where she uses her story as a domestic violence survivor along with Biblical references to help all women remember their worth.

I would like to dedicate this devotional to my grandmother Dorothy Douglas. She is one of the main reasons I believe in God and had me memorize my first Bible chapter, Psalms 23. I would also like to acknowledge my husband, Andrew Pettis who was very instrumental in me finding my voice in the midst of my story.

KRYSTAL HENRY

I am an evangelist and the first lady of Power of the Gospel Ministries in Dallas, TX since 2000. Breast Cancer is a Silent Killer, but I will not be a Silent Survivor of Triple Negative Breast Cancer. I am that foolish thing that God uses to confound the wise!

I dedicate this to every reader that entrusts their hearts to this book. May you be refreshed, enlightened, endowed, encouraged, and enabled to go further than you ever thought or asked in Jesus name.

LAURRY MANUEL

Laurry Manuel is a native of Houston, Texas. The youngest of three children, she gave her heart to Christ at the tender age of 15. She is an amazing mother to two beautiful daughters. She enjoys spending time with her family, crocheting, and interpreting for the deaf and hard of hearing. Laurry's amazing life experiences have not only strengthened her walk with Christ but many of those of whom she has come in contact. Laurry is a licensed cosmetologist and owner of Let's Keep U Kute hair salon in Cedar Hill, Texas.

I dedicate this to my daughters, Kyra and Kayla. Be the beautiful, strong leaders God has ordained you to be.

SCHERRIE JONES

Scherrie Jones is the beautiful wife of Marlon Jones, her husband of fourteen years. They have four wonderful children—Paiton, Marlon III (Tre), Patrick, and Reese and live in Fort Worth, Texas.

Scherrie is an educator, involved and active parent, community engagement leader, and a pastor's wife.

She has earned her Bachelor of Arts degree in Criminal Justice and Sociology from Dillard University. She also earned her Master of Education in Educational Leadership from Dallas Baptist University. She is passionate about education and enjoys working with children and has spent several years teaching children in various levels in elementary school. She serves on the Racial and Equity Committee for Fort Worth ISD. She also serves on the Site Based Decision Making Committee as parent liaison at her children's elementary school. She leads Hello Beautiful!, a ministry she created to assist women and young girls in having fun together, having Godly ambition, noticing their value, and most of all helping others reach their full potential.

I would like to dedicate this work to my husband and my wonderful four children for enjoying amazing adventures with me, sharing their lives with me, making me laugh, for filling my heart with love, and for practicing unconditional love.

SHAWANA L. FOSTER

I am a native of Oklahoma and married to Elder David C. Foster Jr. of Sacramento Ca. God has gifted me in many areas. I am a Fashion Designer of several lines—Inspirational Dance wear, Purse line: Wannie Totes, and I alter and design Wedding dresses, but my passion is ministering in Praise and Worship but I keep my spirit open for God to pour in more.

This is dedicated to David, Christina, and Cherub. For we have endured much pain and struggle and we survived.

SHERLYN WARNER

Sherlyn Warner currently works in education and is the mother of a 10-year-old daughter named Noa. She has over 20 years of work experience, training, knowledge in performing administration and analytical functions, social-media, public relations, implementation of legislative and civil change for community-based and non-profit organizations. She has strong communicator skills (verbal and written) and 15 years public speaking experience. A customer- and client-focused individual, Sherlyn is a military veteran honorably discharged.